The World's Greatest Civilizations: The History and Culture of Ancient Sparta

By Charles River Editors

Bronze monument of Spartan King Leonidas at Thermopylae

About Charles River Editors

Charles River Editors was founded by Harvard and MIT alumni to provide superior editing and original writing services, with the expertise to create digital content for publishers across a vast range of subject matter. In addition to providing original digital content for third party publishers, Charles River Editors republishes civilization's greatest literary works, bringing them to a new generation via ebooks.

Signup here to receive updates about free books as we publish them, and visit charlesrivereditors.com for more information.

Introduction

Ancient Sparta

"The walls of Sparta were its young men, and its borders the points of their spears." – attributed to King Agesilaos

There have been no shortage of great warrior societies in history, including the Romans, Mongols, Macedonians, and Vikings, the list goes on. Yet one humble city in particular, nestled in a valley near the Eurotas river in the Greek region of the Peloponnese and once ridiculed as little more than a cluster of villages inhabited by uncouth shepherds, produced the most famous warrior elite the world has ever known.

The most unique city-state in Ancient Greece was Sparta, which continues to fascinate contemporaneous society. It is not entirely clear why Sparta placed such a great emphasis on having a militaristic society, but the result was that military fitness was a preoccupation from birth. If a Spartan baby did not appear physically fit at birth, it was left to die. Spartan children underwent military training around the age of 7 years old, and every male had to join the army around the age of 18.

The Spartans, whose carefully constructed approach to warfare and – there is no other word for it – *Spartan* way of life, earned the grudging admiration of all of Greece and succeeded in establishing themselves in the years following the reforms of the semi-legendary ruler Lycurgus as the greatest military force in all of Hellas. Athens might have the mightiest fleet and the greatest cadre of philosophers and dramatists, Thessaly might have had the most vaunted cavalry, and the great city-states of Argos, Thebes and Corinth all had their own claims to fame, but on the battlefield the Spartan phalanx stood without peer. So feared were they in Greece that their very appearance on the battlefield could cause entire enemy armies to flee in terror, and in one of history's most famous battles, 300 Spartan warriors headed a combined Greek force which held off the hundreds of thousands of Persian warriors of Xerxes's invading army for three days at Thermopylae, inflicting an estimated 20,000 casualties upon them before dying to the last man rather than retreating.

Sparta will forever be known for its military prowess, but they had lives off the battlefield as well, and their way of life was also unique. For example, Spartan females were formally educated, which was a rarity among the city-states, and the Spartan way of life was entirely dependent on a class of indentured servants known as the helots. Yet the Laws of Lycurgus, which ordered all Spartans to disregard art (with the exception of song, which the Spartans prized, and some forms of music and poetry), to distrust philosophy, and to abhor excess in all things, were designed to create the perfect warrior society, and they did. As a result, the Spartans became notorious for "Laconic phrases"

The World's Greatest Civilizations: The History and Culture of Ancient Sparta comprehensively covers the history and culture of the famous Greek city-state, looking at their religious, political, and military past, and examining all their accomplishments. Along with historic artwork depicting important people, places, and events, *The History and Culture of Ancient Sparta* will bring readers up to speed on Ancient Sparta today.

The World's Greatest Civilizations: The History and Culture of Ancient Sparta

About Charles River Editors

Introduction

Chapter 1: Sparta's Military and Tactics

Anyone with even the most basic understanding of Sparta is aware that Sparta's single most important defining characteristic was its army. Throughout the centuries, the Spartan navy, aside from a brief period of supremacy under Lysander's tutelage, was a relatively insignificant force, reflecting the importance the Spartans placed on the army. Sparta was the quintessential warrior society, and for over two centuries they were regarded as the finest fighters in all of Greece, if not the world.

However, a common misconception is that all Spartan warriors were as fearsome, or trained to such a peak of physical and martial perfection, as the Three Hundred who faced Xerxes's horde at Thermopylae. In actual fact the Three Hundred were not merely Spartans but *Spartiates*. Spartiates they constituted a small ruling elite whose numbers were replenished, barring extreme measures, only by direct inheritance. They were at their highest during Sparta's heyday in the Persian Wars (around 9000 men) and at their lowest during Sparta's nadir in the build-up to the Roman conquest (around 400). It was the Spartiates who underwent the ruthless training of the *agoge*, the Spartan military academy, and who formed the soul and backbone of the army and Sparta itself. They referred to themselves as the *homoioi*, or Peers, because each of them could speak his mind freely before the Kings or the Ephors without fear of reprisals. In accordance to the laws of Lycurgus, each Spartiate kept a *cleros*, or farm, to support himself.

The Spartiates fought exclusively as armored heavy infantry, or hoplites, and the best of them joined either the *krypteia*, the somewhat unsavoury secret society whose task was to keep the unruly helot population in check, or the *hippeis* the elite bodyguard of three hundred who protected the King. In addition to the Spartiates, there were the *perioikoi*, those "living around", who also fought for much of Sparta's history as armored infantry. And of course thre were the helots, who accompanied the Spartan army to war both as light infantrymen and skirmishers and as personal squires to the Spartiates.

The *agoge*, the military training that Spartan youths who wished to be known as Spartiates had to undertake from ages 7-20, is considered one of the harshest, most brutal and physically demanding boot camps in history, and many young men did not survive it. One of the ordeals of the *agoge* involved a roughly 8 mile cross-country run, which the boys in training were expected to complete while holding a full mouthful of water without spilling or drinking it. One of the boys, drinking his ration of water accidentally when he stumbled, is said to have bitten through his own tongue and, filling his mouth with blood, spat it out at the feet of his instructors, which gives an idea of the standard set by the *agoge*. It was firmly affixed in the Spartan mind that war should be a respite from training, and accordingly they strove to make training more miserable and back-breaking than war could ever be.

To alleviate this misery, and provide instruction to the young boys, each of them was assigned an older Spartiate mentor. This has given rise to the popular academic theory that the Spartans had institutionalised pederasty, with the Spartan warriors literally loving each other. However, Xenophon, Plutarch and Aristotle all refute this idea, something they would have had no reason to do if the relationship between the boys and mentors had not been platonic, because pederasty was a fairly common and established practice in Greece.

At age 20, the trainees graduated from the *agoge* and became full Spartiates and *homoioi*, and they were allowed to dine at common messes ("*sissitia*") with other men until age 30, at which point they were forced to marry (if they had not already) and could now live and dine with their families. Spartiates were expected to be in full service until age 30 at least, and in active reserve until 60 or even 75.

Most historians believe that the hoplite became the dominant infantry soldier in nearly all the Greek city-states around the 8th century B.C. Hoplites were responsible for acquiring their own equipment, so not every hoplite might have been equally armed, but considering the style of warfare, they needed as much uniformity as possible.

Like most infantry outside of Greece, the hoplites also carried spears, but while the Persian weapons were short and light for example, the Greek spears were thick shafts anywhere between seven and nine feet long. These spears were topped by a 9-inch spearhead, with a "lizard-sticker" buttspike at the bottom which could be used as a secondary spearhead if the main weapon was snapped off, or to plant the spear upright when at rest. Each hoplite also carried a shortsword, designed specifically for thrusting in the close confines of a melee (the Spartan weapon, the *xiphos,* was so short as to be virtually a dagger, its blade barely over a foot long). Unlike the Persian infantry, the hoplites did not carry bows. Though the Greeks did employ light infantry, in the form of slingers, javelineers and archers, their role was extremely secondary to that of the heavy infantry.

This was largely due to the armor which each hoplite wore into battle, which consisted of bronze greaves covering the wearer from ankle to knee, a skirt of leather or quilted linen to protect the groin area, and a heavy breastplate made either of bronze or quilted linen under overlapping bronze scales. To protect their heads, the hoplites wore the famous helmet that is perhaps their most iconic feature, a full-face bronze helmet with high flaring cheek-pieces and a thick nasal that obscured and protected their faces completely, topped by a horsehair crest that added another foot to their height. Helmets were worn front-to-back for line infantry and sideways for officers, to make them more recognizable to their own troops in the heat of battle.

Armored from head to foot in iron and bronze, the hoplite was the tank of his age, but the most important feature of his equipment was undoubtedly his shield. Weighing in at over 30 pounds, the *hoplon* or *aspis* was a great wooden bowl over three feet in diameter, made of heavy oak fronted with bronze and covering each hoplite from knee to neck, as well as providing a significant overlap with the shields of his companions in the battle-line. There could be no standing off and engaging the enemy at a distance with the Greek hoplites carrying shortswords and thrusting spears, and because of the weight of their equipment (which was up to 70-90 pounds all told).

19th Century illustration of a Hoplite

For the Spartans, a hoplite was only as strong as the hoplite next to him; without hoplites on the sides, both flanks were exposed, and heavy infantry units are not mobile. Thus, they implemented the phalanx formation, one of history's most important military innovations. The phalanx was a line of infantry as wide across as the battlefield dictated, anything from five to 30 men deep, with each rank of men officered by a veteran. The formation also included an additional, expert file-closer at the back of each file, to keep the formation cohesive.

The phalanx advanced slowly to maintain its tight formation and unit cohesion, speeding up in unison just before reaching combat. The vast hoplite shields overlapped one another significantly, forming an uninterrupted wall of oak and bronze over which the first rank, while holding out their shields, would use their short swords to stab at the enemy in front of him, while the ranks immediately behind the first rank would slash at enemies with their spears over the top of the first line. Because each soldier's right flank was shielded by his companion's shield (all shields were strapped to the left arm, to preserve the integrity of the formation; left-handed fighters did not exist), the phalanx, especially in the case of less well-trained units, had a tendency to edge to the right, which the Greeks countered by placing their elite troops to the right as a bulwark. The rows in back of the first line would also use their shields to help hold up the hoplites in the front and help them maintain their balance. The formation and method of attack was designed to physically overpower the enemy and scare them, lowering their morale. The phalanx as a fighting unit fell out of favor by the height of the Roman Empire, but the principles behind it remained in use for subsequent infantry formations lasting past the American Civil War. As the Greeks relied on the hoplite to defend other hoplites and concentrate their attack, infantry units in the gunpowder age relied on concentrated gunfire to stun and scare the enemy. And as military commanders learned time and again throughout the ages, if soldiers were not packed shoulder to shoulder in a tight formation, they were far more likely to flee.

Ultimately, though this is a subject of some contention, much of the consensus argues that the main strength of the hoplite phalanx was its utter inexorability when it operated as a cohesive, immaculately drilled unit – an unstoppable juggernaut which relied less on the initial clash of shield-walls (hoplites never advanced at a run, to preserve their formation) than on the relentless pushing force of their advance to shatter the enemy formation. Because only the first three ranks could bring their weapons to bear, the fight quickly degenerated into a shoving scrum until one side broke, which generally decided the outcome of the battle.

The Spartans, due to the ferocity of their training and the intensity of their drill, were peerless at phalanx warfare. They were Greece's only full-time soldiers, with most other cities fielding citizen militias instead, so they avoided the traditional hoplite problem of edging to the right, into the "shadow" of their rankmate's shield. This edging meant that undisciplined formations often found themselves outflanked, and all armies, including the Spartans, fielded their elite unit (in the Spartans' case the *hippeis*) to the far right to keep the line steady. The left was traditionally reserved for the *skiritai*, the Spartan rangers, who considered it their post of honour.

The Spartan army itself was, during its heyday, strictly organised and officered, divided into five to seven *lochoi* (battalions) of a thousand men, each of which was divided into four *pentekostyes*, which in turn were dived into sixteen *enomotai* of 32 men, the platoon of the Spartan army, commanded by an *enomotarches*. Depending on the period, two to four *lochoi* formed a *mora*, or regiment, which was commanded by a *polemarch*, the Spartan equivalent of a general. *Enomotai* were usually drawn from members of the same *sissitia*, ensuring the soldiers in the ranks trained and relaxed together as friends as well as fighting together, and were generally comprised of a mixture of both young and inexperienced men and veteran soldiers. Because the Spartans had little time for light infantry, and virtually none for cavalry, these roles were relegated to helots and allies.

It was the hoplite infantrymen, forged in the pitiless furnace of the *agoge* and tempered in battle, who were the foundation of Spartan society and the main reason for Spartan supremacy, and the Spartans knew this and cherished them.

Chapter 2: The History of Sparta from the Bronze Age to the Roman Empire

Traditional ancient hoplite helmet

"Demaratus, being asked in a troublesome manner by an importunate fellow, 'Who was the best man in [Sparta]?' answered at last, 'He, Sir, that is the least like you.'" – Plutarch, *Life of Lycurgus*

It would be impossible to overstate the influence Ancient Sparta and their warriors had on history. Though they are remembered within the context of Ancient Greek history, and for battles like Thermopylae and the Peloponnesian War, their way of fighting extended far beyond the Greek peninsula. Both their fighting ethos and their tactics have been passed down to subsequent generations.

The spectacular valor and prowess of the Spartan warriors so impressed the Persians that Spartan mercenaries became the backbone of many Persian armies in the centuries to come, and until the advent of the Macedonian Phalanx under Philip of Macedon and later Alexander the Great, and barring a brief Theban predominance under the brilliant generals Pelopidas and Epaminondas, there is no doubt that the Spartans were, quite simply, the greatest heavy infantry in the world. Yet it was not merely their magnificence on the battlefield, or their spectacular prowess in the sacred games at Olympia, that were so admired by their contemporaries. Rather, it was the philosophy of which these athletic and martial achievements were the product that inspired and continues to inspire thousands of people to this day: the Spartan way of life, where life's pleasures were enjoyed in the simplest way possible, eschewing all luxury, superfluity and vice, is a deeply fascinating ideal and one which is often cited as the pinnacle of virtue.

In the millennia to come, great generals and armies have adopted Spartan custom, and to this day their influence remains a powerfully felt force in many modern military establishments. The novel *Gates of Fire*, written by an ex-Marine and detailing the Spartan exploits at Thermopylae, is required reading at West Point; the badge of the British Special Forces Reconnaissance Regiment is a Spartan helmet surmounted by a sword; and many American soldiers in Afghanistan go into war with patches on their arms bearing the Greek inscription "MOLON LABE" – the words spoken to the Persian envoy at Thermopylae by Leonidas, who, when enjoined to order his men to lay down their weapons, replied with the pithy phrase, "come and get them". Yet for all this, perhaps the greatest testament to the Spartans may be found in the archaeological evidence unearthed by scholars on the site of where their ancient city stood. Try as they might, archaeologists could find no evidence of city walls, which ringed every other city-state in Greece, save for a small concentric wall which seems to have lasted less than half a century. The reason for this is simple: barring one abortive attempt, they were never built. As Lycurgus is said to have noted, "A city is well-fortified which has a wall of men instead of brick."

Statue of Leonidas with the inscription MOLON LABE

Prehistory to 7th Century B.C.

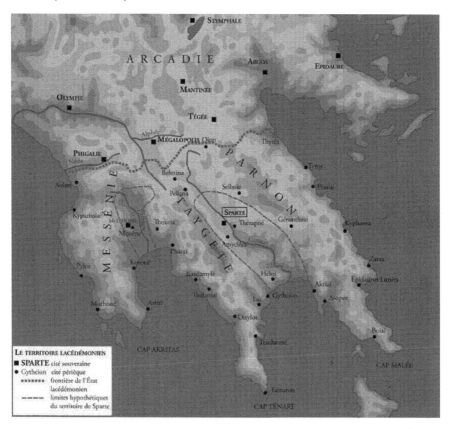

According to the archaeological evidence uncovered on the site of ancient Sparta (and its immediate surroundings within the valley of the Eurotas), the region was inhabited at least from the Neolithic Period. The valley of the Eurotas constituted a natural strongpoint, as it was (and to some extent still is) a wide, fertile plain, watered by the Eurotas river and ringed with high, virtually impassable peaks that could only be penetrated by a handful of high, easily defensible passes, something which contributed greatly to Sparta's subsequent ascendancy. However, the original settlers appear to have been supplanted by what Herodotus refers to as the Dorian Invasion, when a fair-haired tribe from Macedonia supposedly descended into southern Greece and the Peloponnese, displacing the local population approximately half a century after the Trojan War. According to several prominent scholars, however, Herodotus's evidence is to be discounted as he wrote based on myth and hearsay, hundreds of years after the events he accepts as creditable fact.

Another theory is that the Dorian people were already present in large numbers within the Peloponnese but formed the backbone of a downtrodden servile class, and the Dorian Invasion was actually an uprising which led to the overthrow of the established rulers. Whichever theory is correct, however, what is certain is that, in their own minds, the Spartans were fiercely Dorian, spoke a Doric dialect, and considered themselves quite distinct from their Attic rivals from Athens.

As Homer suggests, it is likely that during the period of Mycenean predominance, which ended around approximately 1200 B.C., Sparta was subservient to Mycenae – as evidenced by the fact that Menelaus, king of Sparta, is required to pay tribute to his older brother, and supreme ruler, Agamemnon. However, following the collapse of Mycenae, archaeological evidence suggests a marked increase in the size of the four settlements which would eventually be assimilated into classical Sparta, a consequence both of apparent stability in the area and the fact that the valley of the Eurotas was by far the most fertile region in the Peloponnese, thus promoting agrarian expansion and a population boom.

Between roughly 1000 and 800 B.C. Sparta seems to have enjoyed a period of prosperity and growth, although historical sources from this period are non-existent and what was written down about it subsequently is, to put it charitably, sparse. What does appear certain is that between the 8th and 7th centuries B.C., Sparta suffered from a period of intense factionalism which led to a state of quasi-lawlessness and disunity. It is likely that this was a cause of the assimilation of four villages – Pitana, Limnai, Mesoa and Konoura – into the polity of Sparta, a process which evidently caused significant issues with the stability of the Eurotas valley region as each village had its own "kings" and entrenched ruling classes, all vying for supremacy in the new social order. It is a popular theory that Sparta's famous "double kings" system, whereby two monarchs (much like the subsequent Roman consuls) shared equal amounts of power so that, if one were killed in battle, the Spartan state would not find itself leaderless, originated during this period: the villages of Pitana and Mesoa had formed a faction which vied for control of Sparta with Limnai and Konoura, and it seems likely that the leaders of these two twin factions eventually became Sparta's dual monarchs. However, this period of instability is notable chiefly because, according to legend, it was during this time (according to Herodotus and Thucydides, during the reign of King Charillos) that Lycurgus the Law-Giver rose to power.

Bust of Lycurgus

It is hard to separate the myth of Lycurgus from the real man, and indeed many scholars doubt he ever even existed. However, to the Spartans, he was a very real figure indeed. Far from being a mythological being that was most likely a figurehead for a collection of reformers and monarchs, he was the foundation of all that it meant to be a Spartan. His famous reforms established the bedrock of classical Sparta, enjoining (among other things) all Spartan males who possessed a farm whose wealth was sufficient to maintain their upkeep to devote themselves solely to the practice of war and the inextricably linked field of athletics. Though the Olympics of ancient Greece were a harmonious event during which time no war could be waged, all events remained fiercely bellicose; the armoured sprint, the foot race, wrestling, javelin-throwing, discus throwing, boxing and the pentathlon were all meant to prepare a man for battle.

Lycurgus also supposedly promoted clean, simple living and the abandonment of all luxuries both personal and of the state, allowing the Spartans the one "foible" of growing their hair long. The argument in favor of these prohibitions was that no other adornment made a good-looking man more handsome or an ugly one more terrifying.

Lycurgan reforms also granted Spartan women an unprecedented amount of freedom, and though they had no formal political power, they were encouraged to speak their minds openly in public assembly.

Uniquely among other Greek states, the Spartans also lacked a currency. Sparta was virtually economically self-sufficient in terms of produce and craft expertise, and the Laws of Lycurgus stated that currency debased men, who would then in turn only seek its amassment; better, then, to dispose of it altogether. More controversially, the reforms also encouraged the widespread exposure of newborn children; male children of Spartan citizens in particular. If a baby looked to be too sickly, weak or malformed to endure the trial of the *agoge* (the Spartan military academy and allegedly another of Lycurgus's innovations), then the baby was as often as not abandoned to die.

The Laws of Lycurgus, regardless of whether they were the product of a single man's imagination or the result of a drawn-out political process, gave Sparta much-needed stability. In the wake of the quelling of its internecine wars, Sparta began to devote itself to the subjugation of its neighbouring territories, and the expansion of its influence throughout the entire Peloponnese. During the aftermath of the Lycurgan reforms, Sparta waged several successful wars against the neighboring (but ethnically distinct) Arcadians, and their fellow Doric Argives. The wars were a brutal affair in which hundreds or perhaps thousands of the defeated are said to have been put to the sword, displaced or enslaved, but the Spartans emerged triumphant. By around 750 B.C., they had added Amyclae, Pharis and Geronthrae to their domains, ensuring control of the entire upper Eurotas valley, in a war that was less about one *polis* (city-state) against the other than it was about one ethnic group attempting to wipe the other out. In this case, the Doric tribes wishing to exterminate the neighbouring Achaeans, who had been the ascendant group, by and large, since before the Trojan War. The success of Spartan arms in this war, and the ruthlessness with which they pursued it, first established the basis for the Spartan tradition of victory, which would in subsequent centuries become so cemented as to be virtually ingrained in both their own psyche and that of all of Greece.

This military predominance was further cemented when, sometime between 750 and 650 B.C., two successive wars were waged by the Spartans against their immediate neighbours, the polity of Messenia. Though the wars were ferocious (the first conflict, according to Tyrtaeus, lasted almost two decades) and bitter, the Spartans eventually emerged as the victors, and this ascendancy of their immediate neighbours led to the birth of the social class known as helots. The helots, who were all of Messenian descent, were indentured serfs (by all accounts, virtually slaves) who were bound to the land they were born on. The helots worked the fields and performed all manner of agrarian and other forms of labour, such as those of armorer or groom, requiring a high level of skill. Most importantly, this system left the Spartans truly free to follow the Lycurgan reforms and devote themselves entirely, in their every waking moment, to training and preparing for battle. According to the ancient Roman historian Plutarch, when the Spartan king Anaxandridas was asked how the Spartans dared to leave their fields in the control of the helots, he explained, "It was not by taking care of the fields, but of ourselves, that we acquired those fields."

Nevertheless, helots weren't exactly ordinary slaves. Though their status was lowly, helots were valued by many of the cannier Spartans, who saw the need to cultivate their allegiance, and helots always assisted the Spartan army in battle. Each armored heavy infantryman, or hoplite, was accompanied by a helot "squire" who also fought as a light infantryman (usually as an archer or javelineer) and helped carry his master's load, repair his *panoplia* (battle-kit) and tend his wounds.

The Spartans came to be wholly dependent on the helots in the years to come, a dependence which, as the Spartans were well aware, was dangerous. In later years, the Spartans became so afraid of a helot revolt, something which occurred frequently enough, that they were forced to prepare a full call-up of their army only with extreme rarity, lest the helots rise up in their absence.

6th-4th Century B.C.

"Stranger, announce to the Spartans that here We lie, having fulfilled their orders." – Epigram for the Spartans of Thermopylae written by Simonides of Ceos

Sometime between 600 and 550 B.C., Sparta was still led by two kings Agasicles and Leon, but by this point the Ephorate, a council of five elders, one from each *deme* of Sparta and with a large share of the executive power, had also been introduced. It was also around this time that Sparta waged a vicious war against the neighbouring city of Tegea, another Arcadian *polis*. Tegea resisted with unprecedented tenacity, even inflicting a serious defeat upon the Spartans at what became known as the Battle of the Fetters, and eventually Sparta was forced – in a sea-change of policy – to desist from its attempts to subjugate the Tegeans and reduce them to helot status. Sparta instead accepted a grudging agreement from the Tegeans to accept Sparta as their *hegemon* (overlord). This stubborn resistance led the Tegeans to acquire a significant amount of fame as warriors, their valour and skill at arms being characterised by ancient Greek historians as being second only to that of the Spartans themselves.

The upshot of the war was that Sparta now gained a valuable ally in ensuring the continued pacification of the restless Messenian territory, and also a buffer between its own dominions and those of the closest rival superpower, the mighty city of Argos. The following decades of Spartan policy were to be shaped by their desire to gain ascendancy over Argos, and in 546 B.C., following the Battle of Champions, Sparta inflicted another serious reversal on the Argives by taking control of the troubled no-man's-land of Cynuria. Cynuria had been a contested territory which stood between Argolis, the Argive sphere of influence, and Laconia, the fledgling Spartan Peloponnesian domain (hence the modern word "laconic", as the Spartans were notorious for being men of few words).

Approximately half a century after the Battle of Champions, in 494 B.C. Sparta launched a mighty expedition under King Cleomenes with the intention of destroying Argos once and for all. The Argives fought back, but their forces were annihilated by the Spartan heavy infantry at the Battle of Sepeia, causing such devastation to the Argive war effort that they effectively became a second-rate power. The Argives were forced to acquiesce to humiliating peace terms. It is said that when Cleomenes was asked why he had spared Argos when it lay prostrated and defenceless before him, he remarked mildly that Sparta needed the Argives – they gave young Spartans something to practice on.

The defeat of Argos established Sparta once and for all as the dominant land power throughout all of Hellas, its armies invincible and its might unquestioned. Other powers, chiefly Athens, might be more dominant at sea, but wherever battle was joined on land, the Spartans were without peer. As Sparta suddenly vaulted into ascendancy, envoys poured in from as far afield as Scythia and Lydia asking for Spartan aid against the Persian Emperor Darius, whose ruthless expansionist policy was poised to threaten half the known world, including Greece herself, for whom Sparta had taken upon itself the self-appointed role of champion.

Ancient Greek depiction of the Persian Emperor Darius

Closer to home, the cities of the Ionian seaboard (Middle-Eastern in terms of geographic location, but Greek in ethnic background and culture) begged for help in their uprising against Darius, while the Greek cities of Megara and Plataea, and later Corinth, declared their loyalty to

Sparta, establishing the beginnings of what later became known as the Peloponnesian League. The League, which would eventually become one of the great political forces in ancient Greece, did not get off to the most successful of starts. The first joint effort by the Peloponnesian League, and the first time Sparta had attempted to assert its political supremacy north of the Isthmus of Corinth, came when the two Spartan kings Cleomenes and Demaratos led an expedition into Attica, Athens's heartland. The Spartans had helped overthrow the Athenian ruler Hippias shortly before, in 510 B.C., and with two political parties, headed by Cleisthenes and Isagoras respectively, vying for supremacy, the situation seemed ripe for political exploitation. The Spartans attempted to back the conservative Isagoras, but the expedition was a complete fiasco: the allies, apprised of the Spartans' intentions, decamped *en masse*, and then the Spartan army itself was riven in two when Demaratos quarrelled with Cleomenes and decided to up the stakes and return home as well. As a result, Spartan credibility was somewhat damaged; rather than being uncontested leaders of the Peloponnesian League, they were now expected to defer to their allies when it came to decision-making, leaving them as a first among equals rather than the overlords they would have likely preferred to be. (As an interesting aside, Demaratos would later be exiled and wound up watching the Battle of Thermopylae from Xerxes's tent.

The league itself stood firm, but its goal seems to have shifted. Rather than ensuring Spartan supremacy, it was now geared towards resisting outside intervention. Cleomenes, it appears, had scented a change in the wind. For hundreds of years, Greece had been riven with factionalism and internal strife, but the time was swiftly approaching when all such differences must be set aside. The might of the Persian empire, the greatest the world had ever seen, was being massed against them by the Emperor Darius. The Persian empire used its unimaginable wealth to equip an army whose numbers were so large they defied understanding. In fact, it's estimated that each province of Persia was capable of raising more men than all the Greek *poleis* combined.

In 491 B.C., following a successful invasion of Thrace over the Hellespont, Darius sent envoys to the main Greek city-states, including Sparta, demanding tokens of earth and water as symbols of submission. Darius didn't exactly get the answer he was looking for. According to Herodotus in his famous *Histories*, "Xerxes however had not sent to Athens or to Sparta heralds to demand the gift of earth, and for this reason, namely because at the former time when Dareios had sent for this very purpose, the one people threw the men who made the demand into the pit and the others into a well, and bade them take from thence earth and water and bear them to the king."

With that, conflict was certain. The hammer-blow was coming, and it struck in 490 B.C., when Darius launched an all-out invasion by attempting to establish a beach-head at Marathon, near Athens. The Greeks, Athens chief among them (all animosity over Spartan intervention just 20 years earlier was apparently forgotten), begged for Spartan help; the mightiest warriors in Hellas, it was declared, must march to Athens's aid immediately. However, not for the last time, the Spartans dithered; according to the Laws of Lycurgus, they were forbidden to march until the waxing moon was full. Accordingly, their army arrived too late. It was the Athenians themselves whose hoplite heavy infantry threw Darius's great army back into the sea at Marathon. After the battle, an Athenian envoy named Pheidippides sprinted the 26.2 miles back to the city on foot, where he announced the city's deliverance before collapsing from exhaustion and dying, giving rise to the famous Olympic event which bears the same name. Conveniently, since all of Greece had been ready to unite in defence of their homes, the Athenian triumph was seen as a Hellenic victory over the Persians rather than a wholly Athenian victory, allowing Sparta to escape with its reputation untarnished.

Despite the victory in the First Persian War, it was felt that, maybe not in the next year or even in the next decade, the Persians would come again. The Spartan king Leonidas was the main advocate of this theory, sustaining it even when Darius died and was succeeded by his son Xerxes in 486 B.C.. Under Leonidas and their other king, Agesilaus, the Spartans waged a series of campaigns in the years following the Battle of Marathon to bring reluctant allies and Persian sympathisers into the fold and ensure a united Greek front would greet all Persian attempts to invade.

That invasion, just as Leonidas had prophesied, came in 480 B.C., when Xerxes, at the head of an army which Herodotus states numbered over a million men, bridged the Hellespont (the Dardanelles straits) via a colossal pontoon bridge and marched his army into Thrace, threatening Greece proper. All eyes turned to the Spartans: the greatest warriors in all of Greece, surely, must lead the defence of Hellas. Yet once again, the Spartans dithered. It is unclear what prompted the Spartan reluctance to take the field. Some historians have suggested that, being chiefly concerned with the Peloponnese, the Spartans wanted to defend the Isthmus of Corinth, and let the rest of Greece fend for itself. Others accept the official Spartan reason that as a deeply religious people they could not ignore the Olympic proscription, in vigour at that particular time of year, that forbade Greek cities from marching in arms.

Whatever the reason, the Spartans could field only a token force: accordingly, they sent an "all-sire" suicide unit of three hundred full Spartiates, notionally the King's bodyguard, under Leonidas, to defend the pass at Thermopylae in north-eastern Greece. These 300 were bolstered by 600 *perioikoi* or "neighbors" (literally "those nearby"), line infantry of lesser prestige from the towns surrounding Sparta, and a further 900 helot light infantrymen, one for each hoplite. They were also joined by between 3,000-5,000 allied Greeks from Corinth, Arcadia, Mantinea, Tegea, Thespiae, Phokis, Locris, and others.

For three days, Leonidas, his Three Hundred, and their allies withstood wave upon wave of Persian attacks, inflicting more than 20,000 casualties upon the enemy. Finally, outflanked and exhausted, they were defeated; Leonidas sent all the allies in retreat save for the remnant of the Three Hundred, but the Thespian soldiers refused to leave, taking up their places beside the Three Hundred. According to Herodotus, during their legendary last stand, after their weapons and armor were smashed and broken the Greeks fought on with nails and teeth before being at last cut down to the last man.

View of the pass at Thermopylae. At the time of the battle, the coastline was roughly where the road is today, and the trees on the left side of the picture would most likely have been absent.

The ideal of Spartan valor, already considered legendary, now became eternal. The following year, in 479 B.C., the Persian forces under General Mardonius advanced into the Greek interior, and by then Xerxes's army had already burned Athens to the ground and savaged much of the Hellenic heartland. But now Mardonius faced a Greek coalition numbering roughly 50,000 men. The backbone of this force, under Pausanias, were 5,000 full Spartiates and 5,000 *perioikoi*. In the ensuing battle, the Persian forces were virtually annihilated, and though this had been a united Greek effort, the credit for the victory was placed firmly on Sparta's doorstep. Their ascendancy was further confirmed later that same year when, during the naval engagement at Mycale, the Hellenic navy (commanded by the Spartan king Leotychides) was responsible for the victory that finally scoured the Persian navy from the seas, a triumph which threatened to obscure the Athenian triumph at Salamis earlier in the war.

However, in the aftermath of Mycale, Sparta was evidently still conflicted about pursuing expansionism outside of the Peloponnese and Greece itself. Thus, they turned down overtures from the Ionian cities for help in their renewed revolt against Xerxes, rudely suggesting that they abandon their cities *en masse* and resettle in Greece, where space would be made for them by uprooting pro-Persian traitors. The Ionians, disgusted, refused to support Pausanias (now in the role of *navarch*, or admiral) in his expeditions against Byzantium and Cyprus and instead turned to Athens for help, which the seafaring power was pleased to provide. The seeds of Athenian and Spartan rivalry, seeds which would eventually blossom into the worst war in Greece's history, had been sown.

In the wake of the Persian War, Sparta suffered a serious of grievous setbacks. Tegea rebelled in 473 B.C., and their formidable army put up a viciously spirited resistance against the Spartan forces. Tegea was also reinforced by funds and troops from Argos, who was finally recovering from the blow dealt to it by Cleomenes and his forces prior to the Persian War.

Though that rebellion was quelled with difficulty, Sparta's woes were compounded when, in 464 B.C., a colossal earthquake devastated the valley of the Eurotas, tumbling buildings all over Sparta and killing hundreds. The calamity was viewed as an act of wrath by Poseidon, known as "earth-shaker" because the Greeks believed he was responsible for earthquakes (in addition to being the God of the Sea). Regardless, the Messenian helots and apparently certain factions of the *perioikoi* took advantage of the chaos and disaffection in the earthquake's aftermath to rise up against the Spartans.

The crisis was so extreme that the Spartans were forced to seek help elsewhere and even resorted to sending envoys to Athens, but the relief expedition under the Laconophile Athenian leader Cimon was a disaster. The Athenians made no secret of their disapproval of the brutality the Spartans were visiting upon fellow Hellenes in their suppression of the rebellion, and fearing that the Athenians would actually ally themselves with the Messenians, the Spartans rudely sent them packing. Athens responded by allying itself with Argos. Meanwhile, Athens was making no secret of its imperialistic ambitions, and under the dynamic leadership of Pericles, it was becoming a serious threat to Spartan supremacy.

Bust of Pericles

The inevitable war broke out in 460 B.C., splitting Greece down the middle and forcing most of the great *poleis* to align themselves with Sparta or Athens. At the time, however, Sparta itself was unable to field a significant force due to being occupied at home with mopping up the helot revolt. That also required leaving much of the Spartan army on standby in case of further uprisings.

The main Spartan achievement in what became later known as the First Peloponnesian War (the prelude to the far more devastating Second Peloponnesian War which followed shortly thereafter) was a victory over Athens at Tanagra in 457 B.C. At that battle, the Spartan army had supported the Boeotians in preserving their independence, but after the victory they decamped, allowing Athens to take over the region anyway. This caused a scandal in Sparta, ending with the exile of the two kings for supineness, and Sparta was forced to call for a somewhat embarrassing five-year treaty with Athens to recover its strength in the wake of the revolt. It has been suggested that it was around this time that some elements of the *perioikoi* were incorporated into the Spartan line infantry to make up for manpower shortage, although this is an issue of some contention. More importantly, Sparta signed a 30 year peace with its old rival Argos, ensuring it was free to pursue hostilities with Athens.

In 431 B.C., war broke out again. Sparta had made no secret of its hostility to Athens in the years following the First Peloponnesian War and had only narrowly been stopped from engaging in another showdown some years before by the intervention of Corinth. Ostensibly due to the Peloponnesian League's desire to support Korkyra and Potidea against rampant Athenian imperialism, the war was chiefly fought because Sparta feared Athenian imperialism, which threatened to overshadow Sparta altogether.

For a decade Sparta and Athens were at loggerheads, with the Spartan king Archidamus leading the Spartan army into Attica, the Athenian heartland, and ravaging the estates and farms there in the hope of bringing the Athenian army to battle. The Athenians, however, retreated behind the Long Walls which linked the city to the harbor of the Piraeus and watched their farms burn, while simultaneously sending their mighty navy to harry the Spartan or pro-Spartan coastline since the Spartan navy was hopelessly outmatched by their triremes. This impasse lasted for a decade until the peace of Nicias was established in 421 B.C.

Both parties, however, were far from satisfied. A mere six years later, when the belligerents had caught their breath, hostilities broke out again. Under the guidance of the tormented military genius and visionary Alcibiades, the Athenians launched a colossal seaborne invasion of Sicily in hopes of taking the city of Syracuse, which at the time was a colony of Corinth. Alcibiades was not notionally in command, but he had amassed so much power that he was practically in overall command, and he had enemies in Athens who were jealous of his ascendancy. Within weeks of the invasion, Alcibiades was recalled to face a fabricated charge of impiety which, if he were convicted of it, would carry the death penalty. Furious at this snub, Alcibiades turned traitor and threw in his lot with Sparta.

Alcibiades

Alcibiades's overwhelming personality meant that he soon established himself as a major policy-driver in Sparta, and he persuaded the Spartans to send Gylippus, a promising general, to aid the Syracusans. Alcibiades also suggested ravaging the Athenian agrarian regions to render them wholly dependent on produce shipped in by their fleet, which was now largely occupied in Sicily. Within a few weeks of arriving in Syracuse with a small force, Gylippus had reinvigorated and revolutionized the demoralized Syracusan hoplites, and soon pro-Spartan and anti-Athenian Greeks were flocking to his banner from all the corners of Hellas.

The Athenian army under Nicias was investing Syracuse from the beach below the headland on which the city stood, but now it was forced to go on the defensive. With reinforcements under

Demosthenes failing to shake the stalemate, and with supplies running out and the army ravaged by disease, the Athenians attempted an all-out attack against a weak spot in the defences but were cut to shreds. Retreating to their encampment, the Athenians tried to break out of the Syracusan encirclement by sea but their fleet was cut to ribbons. Attempting to march out by land, they were denied water in the scorching Sicilian interior and constantly harassed. Eventually the army surrendered. Their leaders were executed and the survivors sent to work in the salt mines among unendurable hardship. It was a blow that virtually broke Athens's spirit and bankrupted its treasury.

In 412, desperate to secure victory over Athens, the Spartans did the unthinkable and, in a move that would have had Leonidas and the Three Hundred rolling over in their graves, allied with the Persians. They sent Alcibiades, who had by now succeeded in alienating himself with the Spartans too, to conduct a liaison with the wife of King Agis and negotiate with Tissaphernes, the governor of Asia Minor. They agreed to sell out the Ionian Cities in return for a fleet and advisors. The promised ships, men and treasure, however, were few and far between, and the Persian Emperor began to suspect something was afoot. Sending his brother Cyrus to replace Tissaphernes in 407 B.C., the Emperor discovered that Alcibiades had been acting as a double agent for Athens for the previous four years.

Alcibiades was replaced by his nemesis Lysander, a brutal, unscrupulous and wholly competent man who, with Persian gold, turned the Spartan fleet into an instrument of war to rival the Athenian one. In 406 B.C. he defeated Alcibiades (who had returned to Athens) at Notium, forcing him into exile again. And though he was replaced by the less effective Callicratidas, who suffered an Athenian defeat at Arginusai, Lysander had guaranteed Spartan ascendancy to the point where the Spartans felt comfortable offering peace terms. The terms, though generous, were refused by the demagogues who had taken power in Athens after Alcibiades. These Athenians vowed they could defeat Sparta in the face of all evidence.

As hostilities resumed, the Spartans turned to Lysander once more. Though he could not serve as *navarch* again due to the rules governing appointment to that office, he was made admiral in all but name, serving instead as vice-admiral and once again reinvigorating and reconstituting the fleet with Persian gold and mercenary manpower. In 404 B.C. the Spartan navy destroyed the Athenian fleet at Aegospotami, then rolled up the Athenian coastal empire on his way to Athens. Upon overthrowing the pro-Athenian governments of all the *poleis* which stood in his path, Lysander began blockading Athens itself. In the face of this catastrophe, the Athenians were forced to sue for peace, though Lysander and the Spartans treated them with scorn. Eventually, an agreement was reached: total capitulation. Athens would destroy its long walls, renounce all claims on its empire, and keep only its own ancestral lands. Starving, bankrupt and war-weary, the Athenians had no choice but to accept.

Bust of Lysander

When the Athenian political establishment all but disintegrated in the wave of disaffection and despair that followed the acceptance of the Spartan terms, Lysander installed a group of oligarchs commonly known as the Thirty. Pro-Spartan to the bone, they ruled Athens as a virtual dictatorship with the help of a Spartan garrison, murdering pro-democratic spokespeople and any who dared speak out against the regime. Nevertheless, while Lysander was busy setting up Decarchies (oligarchies led by ten men) throughout the former Athenian colonies, Boeotia, Corinth and Elis became openly defiant, providing refuge to Athenian political exiles.

Boeotia eventually went one step further, launching an all-out attack against Athens with the support of Athenian pro-democratic exiles, partially expelling the Spartan garrison from Athens and splitting the *polis* between supporters of the Thirty and of the Ten, a group of ten democratic politicians who had come to the fore during Boeotia's war of liberation. The Spartan King Pausanias was called upon to mediate the situation, and despite Lysander's remonstrances following a period of scrappy fighting, the Ten took control of Athens, with the Thirty fleeing to Eulesis, in Attica, whose population they had wiped out.

Eulesis became a sanctuary for pro-Thirty supporters, but when the Thirty attempted a coup in Athens they were brought to a peace conference under false pretences and massacred. Sparta remained aloof throughout all of this, and displaying signs of the vaunted Spartan honor which had largely been lost during the long and vicious war, ignored Lysander's protests and restored the original governments throughout all of his unilaterally established decarchies. The Spartans could afford to be generous now, since their standing as the strongest polis in Greece was unquestioned.

4th-2nd Century B.C.

In the wake of the Peloponnesian War, the Spartans began to harbor imperialistic ambitions again. They openly supported Cyrus, who had enjoyed a friendly relationship with Lysander, in his attempt to seize the throne of Persia from his older brother Artaxerxes, and even though he was killed at Cunaxa the Spartans used an appeal for help from the Ionians (so often previously rebuffed) and invaded Anatolia. However, their army was crushed by Artaxerxes at Cnidus in 394 B.C., apparently causing a sigh of relief from the Ionian cities who felt Spartan rule would be even more oppressive than subjugation to Persia.

This defeat was rendered less bitter by the fact that King Agesilaus succeeded in defeating the Corinthians and Boeotians at Coronea that same year. Corinth and Boeotia had been rendered hostile when Sparta, using a paper-thin pretext, had invaded their territory at Lysander's urging two years before. The expedition had been led by Lysander and Pausanias, but when Lysander was killed at Haliartus fighting the Boeotians, Pausanias (probably giving thanks inwardly that Sparta was rid of its most interventionist leader) made peace and retreated, an act which forced him into exile. Concurrently, war broke out against a coalition composed of Thebes, Athens, Corinth and Argos, all determined to put an end to Spartan hegemony, now backed by Persia in retaliation for the invasion of Anatolia. Though Sparta was victorious virtually everywhere on land, its armies could not successfuly prosecute the war since its fleet was destroyed by a Persian mercenary fleet at Cnidus. The lack of naval power led to the Athenians raiding the defenceless Spartan coast for the first time since the Peloponnesian War.

In 387 B.C., threatened with Artaxerxes' wrath for having invaded Persian territories, the Spartans somewhat ignominiously ceded Cyprus and the cities of the Asia Minor seaboard to Persia in exchange for Greece's continued independence and the permission to wage war on those who they felt were infringing the treaty. Backed by Persian treasure and influence once again, Sparta now set about subjugating Hellas. Any *polis* whose government was contrary to Spartan policy was forced to change its politicians or face annihilation, and while the Spartan-led Peloponnesian league endured, the Boeotian League and the Chalkidian League were disbanded (the latter after fierce fighting) and their *poleis* enrolled into the Peloponnesian league, willingly or not.

Despite this apparent position of supremacy, Sparta was actually rotting from within. The Spartiate warriors who constituted the backbone of the political establishment and the flower of the army had shrunk in number by almost 80%, killed off by decades of near-continued war. Since their rank was hereditary, there were none to take their place, no matter how much the ranks were bolstered by *perioikoi* and, later, by *neodamodeis*, the "newly-enfranchised" helots granted special status and permitted to stand in the battle-line as armored heavy infantry. In 382 B.C. this rot became apparent when, in a double blunder, the Spartan general Phoebidas led an army into the Kadmeia (the Theban equivalent of the Acropolis) and set up a pro-Spartan puppet government there in violation of the peace of 387 B.C.. When Thebes rose up in rebellion, the Spartans also launched an attack on Athens, whose position was questionable. The attack not only failed but drove Athens into open alliance with Thebes. Sparta suffered a double defeat, on land at Tegyra and on the sea at Naxos, and saw its position of supremacy grievously threatened by the recreation of the Theban-led Boeotian League and a resurgent Athenian Empire.

Scrappy fighting continued for almost a decade, until the Spartans attempted to pacify the situation in 371 B.C. The Thebans, however, met these proposals with a flat-out refusal. Infuriated at their stubbornness, the Spartans sent an army of 11,000 men, including a full complement of Spartiates under King Cleombrotus, to crush the Thebans. The two armies met on the plain of Leuktra in 371 B.C. and, incredibly, the Spartans were utterly defeated, almost single-handedly destroying their reputation as the predominant land warriors in Hellas. Cleombrotus was killed, along with thousands of his men, and for the first time in memory the Thebans were treated to an incredible sight: Spartans in full flight. The Theban general Epaminondas, who was chiefly responsible for the victory at Leuktra thanks to his new Oblique Order (a revolutionary phalanx formation), had just ensured a Spartan decline.

Epaminondas

In 370 B.C. Sparta attempted to preserve a toehold of influence in Arkadia by invading, but the Arkadians, knowing which way the wind blew, promptly asked for assistance from Thebes. A Theban army under Epaminondas was promptly sent to the Arkadians' aid and, after having liberated the region, began marching toward Sparta proper. For reasons unknown, Epaminondas decided not to march toward the city itself, perhaps realizing that such an unprecedented threat to their very city would drive the Spartans to feats of Herculean desperation. Instead, he diverted his army toward the helot capital of Messene and began liberating vast tracts of Messenia, ensuring an all-out helot uprising and then fortifying the city so the Spartans could not retake it.

Worried by the newly ascendant power of Thebes, several of Sparta's erstwhile enemies, including Mantinea and Athens, made common cause with the Spartans. In 362 the Boeotian League, led by Theban forces, faced this impromptu coalition at the Battle of Mantinea. Though the Spartans were once again defeated, Epaminondas himself was killed in the hour of victory. A peace was sought, but Sparta snubbed the negotiations, which decreed Messenia independent. Hemmed in by enemies – Argos, Messenia, Arkadia – on all sides, Sparta was in no position to pursue imperialistic policies, and indeed the city's very survival was threatened.

Because of this, Sparta was in no position to assist the Thebans, Athenians, and other Greek powers in their attempt to stop the invasion by the newly arisen superpower, Macedon, led by Philip II and his son Alexander the Great. The Macedonian invasion culminated with the great battle at Chaeronea in 338 B.C. Spartan warriors might well have helped turn the tide, but they were ringed by enemies and none could march to battle. In the aftermath, the Spartans refused to join the League of Corinth, an anti-Persian Hellenic coalition with Philip as *hegemon*, but Philip, unruffled, simply left Sparta surrounded by bellicose and hostile enemies and carried on with his business.

Sparta might have been humbled, but she was hardly broken. When Philip decided to threaten the Spartans, warning them that if he were forced to enter Laconia in arms he would raze Sparta to the ground, the Spartan envoys replied simply, "If". Alone among the Greek city-states, Sparta refused to join the expedition that Alexander, in the wake of his father's death, launched to destroy the Persian empire, a snub Alexander never forgot.

Seven years later, while Alexander (now *hegemon* of the League of Corinth in addition to a host of recently-acquired titles, including Emperor of Persia) was warring in the East, Greece rose up in all-out rebellion. A coalition, headed by Sparta itself, marched against the Macedonian garrisons scattered throughout the country, overthrowing several before laying siege to Megalopolis in 331 B.C. Battle was joined before the city's walls between the Macedonian army left behind by Alexander, commanded by the veteran general Antipater, and the Greek forces under the Spartan King Agis III. As at Chaeronea, however, the Greek hoplites found themselves hopelessly incapable of confronting the relentless machine of the Macedonian phalanx, whose soldiers employed pikes three times as long as the hoplite spears. More than 3,000 Spartans, in the thickest part of the fighting, were killed. The mortally wounded Agis, in the grand tradition of Leonidas and the Three Hundred, ordered his men to abandon him during the retreat so he could buy them some time, and he slayed several of the enemy before he was finally brought down. In the wake of their defeat, Alexander, mindful of their proud history, was merciful to the Spartans, his only condition being that they join the League of Corinth like the other great *poleis*. Even still, during the Lamian War, a renewed Greek uprising against Macedonian rule which followed the conflict at Megalopolis, Sparta remained aloof and continued to do so until Alexander's death.

In the wars of the *diadochii,* the "successors" who tore Alexander's empire apart in their quest for supremacy in the wake of his premature death, Sparta, like many other former Macedonian subject states, recognized an opportunity to reassert its independence. When Demetrius the Besieger, one of the most successful *diadochii,* set about conquering the Peloponnese in 294 B.C. the Spartans attempted to resist. Due to their antiquated equipment and tactics, however, they were defeated twice, and Sparta itself was spared only due to Demetrius's apparent lack of interest and the fact that Sparta did not possess any valuable plunder, since they had no currency or a citadel worthy of that name.

For the following 20 years, Sparta engaged in a series of scrappy internecine wars against other Greek cities in an attempt to re-establish some form of Peloponnesian ascendancy, but their magic had long since vanished and they were defeated repeatedly, even by an undistinguished military power such as the Aetolians. In 272 B.C. Sparta faced an all-out catastrophe when, abetted by the exiled King Cleonymus, Pyrrhus of Epirus invaded the Peloponnese and marched on Sparta itself. The city was only saved thanks to a last-ditch defense in which even the women, children and elderly of the city are said to have taken part.

Sparta then entered a period of flux. Between 264 B.C. and 244 B.C. it fought in a number of skirmishes and small wars in an attempt both to cast off Macedon's yoke and to establish itself as the dominant power in the Peloponnese in the face of growing Aetolian and Achaean opposition. Sparta's woes – and its destiny as an irrelevant former power – seemed to be cemented when the Aetolians raided Laconia and made off with captives which supposedly numbered in the tens of thousands.

Sparta did not take this increasing marginalisation and loss of power lying down, however. In 229 B.C. the Spartan King Cleomenes III besieged Megalopolis, leading to a war with the Achaean League. Despite being outnumbered four to one by the troops of his rival Aratus, Cleomenes succeeded in defeating the Achaeans before leaving most of his army in the field and hurrying back to Sparta with a handful of loyalist troops, where he promptly seized absolute power in a coup, putting four of the five Ephors to death and abolishing the office altogether. Cleomenes then enacted land distribution reforms and conferred the title of Spartiate on new candidates to help beef up the dwindling numbers (now significantly less than a thousand) of full citizens. He also ensured that the land barons, a bare two or three hundred of which possessed the majority of land in Sparta, were stripped of their wealth in favor of a more democratic system. Cleomenes urged a renewal of strict adherence to the Laws of Lycurgus, under the tutelage of his advisor Sphaerus (who was not himself Spartan but, like Alcibiades before him, had made himself "more Spartan than the Spartans"). However, Cleomenes weakened his position by refusing to institute social reform outside of Sparta – instead, he subjugated ruthlessly many newly enfranchised cities which had previously been under Spartan rule.

Cleomenes then turned his attention on Achaea, inflicting a number of defeats upon the Achaean League thanks to financial backing from the Ptolemys of Egypt. Ultimately, however, Aratus allied himself with Macedon and, at the Battle of Sellasia in 222 B.C., crushed Cleomenes and his army. That same year, the King of Macedon, Antigonus III, entered Sparta in arms, a calamity which the city had never experienced throughout its entire history, which led to the re-establishment of the ephorate and the temporary abolishment of the kingship.

Spartan decline continued despite Cleomenes's efforts at reform. Sparta continued to be involved in petty squabbles with neighboring states and coalitions until 207 B.C., when Nabis took power in Sparta. Nabis, who was regarded with loathing by many of his (Roman) biographers, was something of a pirate and a bandit, but also a reformer in the vein of Cleomenes. Like his forebear he attempted to promote a measure of social equality and made changes in the political establishment, but to little avail.

During his reign, the Achaeans abandoned their alliance with Macedon to side with the rising power of Rome, and the Spartans – by default – chose to support Rome's rival, Macedon. In order to keep Argos under more direct control, Philip V, then King of Macedon, ceded it to his newfound ally. This left Nabis, once the Romans had roundly defeated Philip, in the unenviable position of being in contravention of the Roman law that stipulated that all Greek cities should be free. The Romans invaded, besieged Sparta, and forced Nabis to submit to humiliating peace terms which snuffed out Sparta's brief period of ascendancy. Nabis himself was murdered in 192 B.C., and Sparta was forced to endure the humiliation of being forcibly enrolled in the Achaean League.

For approximately 40 years they were forced to bend the knee to the Achaeans until, in 146 B.C., the Romans tired of the constant state of turmoil that characterized Greece. That year the Romans invaded and annexed all of Hellas to the Roman Empire. After 146 B.C. Sparta remained a notionally self-governing enclave and returned, for the most part, to adhering to the previously degraded Lycurgan practices. Their quixotic habits became something of a curiosity in Rome, and many young men of the Roman aristocracy made a point of travelling to Sparta to admire the quaint locals. It was a far cry from the time when being chosen as one of the *trophimoi*, "foster-sons" from other Greek cities, to be inducted into the *agoge* was the highest honour a young Greek nobleman could aspire to. Sparta never recovered in the wake of the

Roman conquest. By the end of the 2nd century B.C., Ancient Sparta had dwindled quietly into irrelevancy.

The ruins of an Ancient Spartan theater

Chapter 3: The Spartan Legacy

From all of this, readers might gain the impression that the Spartan society, with its citizens raised and living in strict adherence to the harsh laws of Lycurgus, was brutal and oppressive. Certainly, in many ways it was. In other respects, however, Spartans (particularly women) enjoyed rights that were unheard of throughout all of Greece.

Athens is known for its democracy, but Sparta also used popular rule. The lion's share of the political power was held not by the dual Kings (who had executive but not legislative roles and could not unilaterally summon the army into the field) but by five Ephors, who served on a yearly basis. The Ephors were chosen by popular ballot from the five principal districts which made up the Spartan polity, and they were always older men. The age cap varies, but generally speaking, no Spartan below thirty could ever serve in a political capacity. Like many posts in Sparta, the term of the Ephorate was one year, and Ephors could not stand for re-election; this was in many ways a positive factor, as it prevented the Ephors from turning to demagogy in an attempt to secure re-election the following year and ensured they would enact only policies they felt were beneficial to Sparta. On the other hand, it meant that deserving candidates could not serve again – Lysander famously circumvented the same legal issue when he wished to serve as *navarch* again by having himself declared vice-admiral instead.

The Ephors, interestingly, were often a violently conservative political force, with the spur of reform and social progression coming not from them but from the hereditary Kings, rather than vice versa. The two kings, who descended from the Agiad and Eurypontid dynasties, had nominally the same amount of power as one another (though the Agiad king was fractionally more important), and for much of Spartan history one would lead the army into the field (with an Ephor at his side to make sure he did not do anything that would contravene the Ephorate's will) while the other remained in Sparta to govern.

In addition to this, the Spartans had two further governing bodies. Sparta had the *Gerousia* or "senate", which was composed of the two kings and a further 28 elders, all Spartiates over 60 who served for life. They also had the *Apella,* or assembly, which was composed of every qualified Spartiate in the city. Unlike in Athens, where politicians or foreign envoys could address the *Apella* directly, in Sparta political proposals and diplomatic overtures had to be made to the Ephors or to certain members of the *Gerousia*, and legislative proposals were brought forth before the *Apella* fully packaged so they could only vote yea or nay.

In addition to these institutions, there were the *hippeis*, who though they had no formal political mandate nonetheless commanded such a high degree of respect that they were in all likelihood influential in swinging the *Apella* one way or another. In fact, even the men who selected the *hippeis* were also politically very powerful. And then there were also the *kripteia*, a shadowy secret society that appears at odds with the tradition of brash martial valour and laconic simplicity that the Spartans cultivated. Still, their function was likely an essential one. Sparta was plagued by helot revolts, and the *kripteia* made the most troublesome ones disappear. To avoid the ritual pollution of murder, the Ephors would declare war on the helots each year, for the express reason of letting the *kripteia* do their dirty work.

Such a rigorous and traditionalist, even brutal, society seems a far cry from the liberal democratic tradition of a city such as Athens, but the truth is that in many respects the Spartans were as progressive as their Athenian rivals. When it came to the role of women in society, they were even more so. Spartiate female children were raised as equals to their brothers until the age of seven, when the boys entered the *agoge*. Spartan girls were encouraged to eat healthily and, rather than eschew the fresh air and the sun, exercise outside as often as possible. Spartan female garments were more revealing than those of other *poleis*, but in a far more innocent way. Spartan beauty was functional, and female cosmetics were forbidden, yet Spartan women were praised as being among the most beautiful in Greece, probably as a consequence of this healthy lifestyle (Helen of Troy herself, after all, was a Spartan).

Spartan women were also allowed and even encouraged to speak their mind in public about any matter that took their fancy, even political and state affairs, something unheard of in other Greek cities. They were also highly educated, being both numerate and literate, which was also virtually unknown for women at the time. Spartan women could also hold land in their own right, administer their husbands' households, and the female Spartan aristocracy became a powerful force of landed gentry in the years following the Peloponnesian War since most of the men had died on the battlefield.

It seems unusual that a society so dependent on martial perfection and powerful men would delegate authority to women or grant them more freedoms than most of the known world at the time. But perhaps the reason is answered by one of Sparta's most famous Laconic phrases, attributed to Leonidas's wife Gorgo. According to Plutarch, "Hence it was natural for them to think and speak as Gorgo, for example, the wife of Leonidas, is said to have done, when some foreign lady, as it would seem, told her that the women of Lacedaemon were the only women of the world who could rule men; "With good reason," she said, "for we are the only women who bring forth men."

Furthermore, as Gorgo's quote suggests, Spartan women also displayed their own brand of courage, which was as highly valued as that of the men who had to face the enemy on the battlefield. As their husbands, sons and brothers marched to war they would watch them depart dry-eyed, saying nothing but the traditional words all Spartan women spoke to their menfolk when handing them their shields before they marched out: "with it or on it!"

As indicated by this outwardly harsh farewell, the life of a Spartan warrior was not an easy one. The Laws of Lycurgus required all Spartiates to devote themselves exclusively to war, and though they also prized reason, logic, learning and singing as much as any other Greek *polis* and had a particular soft spot for comedy (they made laconic wit and the original one-liner popular after all), there is no denying that in many ways their life was a grim and martial one. Though men not in active service were occasionally given furlough to retire to the countryside idyll of their *cleros* and spend time with their families, most of their life was spent training and preparing for war, in the knowledge that failure to do one's duty or cowardice would result at the very least in disgrace and banishment. A Spartiate who abandoned his shield on the field of battle forfeited all his rights and his citizenship and would be scourged out of the city, because the shield was integral to the cohesion of the phalanx as a whole. By abandoning it the Spartiate had endangered not just himself but the entire city – hence "with it or on it".

Nor was reckless valour in the face of the enemy something which the Spartans prized – to them, a lone warrior rampaging ahead of the phalanx in a fury of battle-madness was just as likely to endanger the formation as a coward turning tail and running. Berserk rage was just another form of cowardice to the Spartans. Abandonment of one's senses in the face of battle brought censure rather than praise. Thus Herodotus describes the case of Aristodemos, one of Leonidas's Three Hundred, who was evacuated from Thermopylae the day before the final stand with other casualties because he had been struck by a form of temporary blindness. Aristodemos was so riven with survivor's guilt, not to mention the uncharitable accusations of cowardice that were leveled against him, that at Plataea he fought like a man possessed, but this did nothing to endear him to his fellow Spartiates, who considered his frenzied fighting equally damning.

Ultimately, though there are many aspects of Spartan society that may appear reprehensible – the enslavement of the helots, the *kripteia*, the exposure of children, the constant and stubborn refusal to embrace even the slightest amount of change or countenance a more practical form of expansion than attempting to batter enemies into submission – the simple fact is that their culture never ceases to fascinate or to impress. The very fact that Greeks – often from cities that were rivals of Sparta – considered it the ultimate honour to have their children schooled in the *agoge*, or that the Romans, no un-martial fops themselves, went on pilgrimage to Sparta to see how the world's greatest warriors lived, is a testament to the enduring legacy of their martial spirit. Ultimately, they were the victims of their own inability to change, but perhaps that is for the best. If the Spartans ever compromised their beliefs, they would cease to be Spartan, and people would not still be fascinated by them to this day.

Bibliography

Readers interested in learning more about the Spartans should consult the writings of Thucydides, Xenophon, Plutarch and Aristotle, available in print or for free over the internet as part of the public domain.

For those looking for a more modern take, Paul Cartledge's *The Spartans: An Epic History* is an easy and entertaining read, and Steven Pressfield's *Gates of Fire: An Epic Novel of Thermopylae* makes an excellent fiction companion.

Made in the USA
San Bernardino, CA
20 April 2015